A Way With Words

...Release the Genie Within

Sentiments for all Occassions

By Leonie Featherstone
"The Word Genie"

A WAY WITH WORDS

Author: Leonie Featherstone

First edition copyright © 2008 Leonie Featherstone

All rights reserved. No part of this publication may be reproduced, stored in a retrieval system or transmitted in any form or by any means, electronic, mechanical, photocopying, recording or otherwise, without the prior written permission of the author.

Publisher: Leonie Featherstone
ISBN: 978-0-646-48929-2

Cover Design
Illustrations by Amanda Rattray
Photo by Berit Munro

Contents

Acknowledgements 1
Dedication 3
How To Use This Book 5

Sentiments - Categories
- ❖ Love 10
- ❖ Teacher/Coach 25
- ❖ Mother's Day/Father's Day 29
- ❖ Boss 33
- ❖ Staff 35
- ❖ Christmas 37
- ❖ Christening/Baby 40
- ❖ Moving House 43
- ❖ Bereavement/Loss/Goodbye 45
- ❖ Good luck 51
- ❖ Congratulations/Success/Achievement 54
- ❖ Wedding/Engagement 57
- ❖ Guidance/Inspiration/Friendship 61
- ❖ Thank you 71
- ❖ Happy Birthday 73
- ❖ Business Clients 77
- ❖ 'Mix And Match' Support 79
    - o Nouns 79
    - o Adjectives 80
    - o Verbs 81

Acknowledgements

I inherited my love of writing and poetry from my mother who wrote 'verses' for our birthdays and my Irish grandfather whose romantic poems I cherish.

I have Mum to thank for the birth of this book as she encouraged me to write from a very young age. Childish limericks gradually gave way to more meaningful verse and it wasn't long before I was being called upon to write poems for many and varied occasions.

Life 'excites' me – its magnitude, its opportunities, its beauty and the many wonderful experiences it affords me. Writing – whether it be humour, verse, prose or poetry allows me to express emotions that well up within me when I reflect on the kaleidoscope of people and events that have filled my life.

I am fortunate to have the support of my family and many friends who have encouraged me to continue with my writing. Vernia – thank you for keeping me grounded and for advising me to add verses that 'weren't so mushy'! Scott – you have taught me so much about setting and achieving goals and now, here is 'living proof'! Wendy – without you – this book would still be a dusty manuscript!

I hope my verses are enjoyed by others and may present a 'voice' for those who 'feel as I do' but who may not have the ability to express themselves in the written form.

Enjoy!
Leonie

A way with words – allow the genie to release your feelings and share them with those you love.

To Mum
You are my inspiration,
Thank you for being 'you'!

How To Use This Book

'Genie, dear genie help me today
To express the things I want to say.
Please turn my feelings into words
And allow my message to be heard.'

Welcome to 'A Way With Words'! Throughout my teenage years I discovered that not everyone found it as easy to express their feelings in words as I did. I was constantly being called upon to write a few lines for birthdays, speeches and other events too numerous to list.

It was always such a privilege to be able to be a 'voice' for these heartfelt outpourings. I have written this book to help you deliver your thoughts, straight from your heart, through my words.

I have designed it to be used in a few ways.

1. **Categories.** Simply go through the categories and find the verse that suits your occasion.
2. **Mix and Match.** Check out all the verses in all the categories. Perhaps there is part of one verse from one category that you would like to use along with a part of another verse from a different category. Here you get to be 'part author' by adding and subtracting to suit the occasion.
3. **Change the nouns.** You might like a verse in the Love section that applies to your parents. Just substitute the nouns. (See the page of nouns.) Eg: *'For all the things that you do that make me feel so special – thank you. You are*

the ***love*** *of my life.'* This could become: *'For all the things that you do that make me feel so special – thank you. You are the **rock** of my life.'*

4. **Change the verbs.** You might like the verse for your loved one but the verb might not apply. Just substitute the verbs. (See the page of verbs.) Eg: *'Your smile 'touches' me – you are my 'soul mate'* This could become: *'Your smile **'ignites'** me – you are my 'soul mate'.*

5. **Change the adjectives.** You might like the verse for your Boss but the adjective might not apply. Just substitute the adjective. (See the page of adjectives) Eg: *'You've been a wonderful boss. Thank you for providing **great** conditions and support throughout the year!'* This could become: *'You've been a wonderful boss. Thank you for providing **excellent** conditions and support throughout the year!'*

6. To help you get the best use out of the list of verbs and adjectives so that you can best express yourself - ask yourself these questions.

- ❖ How does this person make me feel? They make me feel valued, loved, cared for
- ❖ How do you feel about this person? Eg I admire them, adore them
- ❖ How would you describe this person? Eg kind, loving, talented

Once you are sure about how you feel about this person and how they make you feel – you will be better able to substitute the right words into the verse pieces you have chosen.

Never be afraid to tell someone how you really feel! Use this book in all its variations and maybe it will even encourage you to venture out to write something totally of your own expression!

Good luck!

Leonie

LOVE

For all the things you do that make me feel so special –
thank you. You are the love of my life.

*****

You are the stars in my sky, the sunrise on my horizon –
you are my world.

*****

We've shared lots of laughs, we've wiped away each other's tears, we've celebrated our successes and we've helped each other through our challenges – you are my partner, my soul mate, my love.

*****

When I'm with you I'm engulfed with a feeling of comfort – safe from danger or harm. I dream I'm lying like an anchored ship - softly cocooned in your arms.

*****

Hold my hand and never let go - together the world will be ours.

*****

You are the world to me – thank you for being a part of my life.

*****

We always know what each other is thinking – we always seem 'in touch'.

*****

Your smile 'touches' me – you are my 'soul mate'.

*****

You are so full of kindness, understanding, love and caring.

*****

I may not always say the right words but I know what I feel – I love you.

*****

You are a beautiful person – from the inside out – so full of understanding and caring, always loving and forever sharing.

*****

You are my best friend and my soul mate. Every day is better because of you.

*****

Throughout the tough times we both learnt how to truly love and that love has grown stronger and stronger.

*****

As I look up into the night sky I wonder where my life would be if I didn't have you as my guiding star.

*****

I'm looking forward to the years ahead and for our dreams to unfold.

*****

I love spending time with you – you are so much fun to be around.

*****

Your friendship is like sunshine dappled through the leaves, its warmth touches every part of me and engulfs me in a drowsy sense of being cared for and loved.

*****

Your friendship is like the reflections on the water – there are two sides to it and by being a friend to me and I to you – we reflect our real worth.
However, unlike the reflections on the water, true friendship cannot be distorted by the wind which ripples across the surface of life.

*****

Twinkling tunes strumming my memory - Troubled thoughts plucking at the strings of my mind - Half hearted tunes run through my consciousness – my mind out of control because you're not here…

*****

My days are so much brighter since you came into my life.

*****

Your name is more than just a name, it touches me deep inside – it means that throughout my life – I'll remember you forever…….

*****

I see your face in the reflections of the stream - I feel your love in the warmth of the sun - As it dapples through the trees I can feel it on the breeze - Filling me full of happiness....

*****

I don't want to leave you but I've got to go – it's hurting me to say goodbye and I want you to know, I'll never forget you – I'll love you always with a special kind of love for the rest of my days.

*****

Love has bound us together like the string on those birthday presents gazed upon longingly and unwrapped with such anticipation.

*****

My heartfelt wish is this, to start a brand new journey - To a destination of unknown dreams - on a path of fresh discovery.

*****

Every day I look upon your 'face' and I smile even though you're far away – I'm hoping my love will travel through the miles and reach into your heart.

*****

I'd love to sit with you again and have this 'distance' ended - to air our thoughts and patch the holes and start a new journey together.

*****

I want to make magical memories and move on from past mishaps on a path that is strewn with laughter and love.

*****

I want to fly on a plane with no destination – I want to wander down a road that never ends – and I want you beside me while I do it….

*****

I want to gaze into your eyes that hold no secrets – I want softly spoken words between us that don't offend – and I want you to want that too

*****

I want to hold a hand that never lets go - I want the touch of fingers that say 'I love you' – and I'm hoping that hand is yours…..

*****

I want your shadow to walk with me wherever I may go…..

*****

Hold me close with no expectations and let us discover life side by side each day

*****

Together we'll see the same bright colours of the rainbow and we'll live and breathe our dreams…. and find our own pot of gold

*****

My love and peace will be yours – our happiness will echo in harmony and you'll be my best friend til we both grow old…

*****

I close my eyes and picture your face - I could drown in that look in your eyes

*****

I'm engulfed in a feeling of comfort – safe from danger or harm - With you by my side I'll have no cause to hide or shrink from the trials that life sends

*****

If you hold my hand and never let go
– the world will be 'ours'

*****

As I look up into the night sky and all the answers that are hidden there - I want you to be standing beside me – sharing those mysteries together

*****

You have been the 'other half' that has made me feel whole.

*****

Let's create more magical moments - let's explore the future days as one.

*****

You are part of the tapestry of my life and will always have a 'home' in my heart

*****

As gently as an angel moves its wings of gossamer threads – you have wound your love around me - and bound my heart and head

*****

An angel's wrapping wings of love around both of you today – hold that love carefully –it is a precious gift to be valued for life.

*****

I seem to smile and laugh more since you've been around. Suddenly the world seems a better place.

*****

It's good to be friends – you're fun to be around
I feel happy when we're hanging out together.
You're cool, you're kind - you're on my mind
You have a way of making me feel special.

*****

Teacher/Coach

Thank you for your support and encouragement throughout the year. I have learnt so much from you.

*****

You have taught me to believe in myself and to stretch beyond what I thought I was capable of. You are a valued part of my success.

*****

You have taught me to 'dare to dream'. Thank you for your support and inspiration.

*****

For all the endless hours you spend sharing your knowledge with me – thank you! Most of all – thank you for believing in me!

*****

Thank you for sharing the keys to knowledge and success. You have introduced me to the excitement of learning!

*****

Thank you for being an integral part of my learning journey. I dedicate my success to you!

*****

Thank you for your patience, your generosity and your understanding. I feel privileged to have been part of your class/team.

*****

You had so many in your class/squad/team and yet you always made me feel like it was all about me. Thank you for sharing your talents, your time and your knowledge to help me be 'the best I can be'.

*****

If there were gold medals for coaching/teaching –you would have a bag full. Thank you for bringing out the best in me.

*****

Mother's Day/Father's Day

For guiding, encouraging me and supporting me through
good times and bad, thank you! You are an awesome
Mum/Dad and I love you very much!

*****

Thanks Mum/Dan for sticking by me even though there must
have been times when you tore your hair out! You have been
an inspirational 'guiding light'
– Happy Father's/Mother's Day!

*****

For caring enough to say 'no' when I wanted you to say 'yes'. For not giving me everything I wanted in life. And for setting an example of what it means to 'live a good life' – thank you!

*****

Mum/Dad – I may not always show it but I appreciate everything you have done for me. Thank you for always being there for me. Enjoy your special day
– you are the best!

*****

For all the times you helped me, encouraged me and stood up for me – thank you! Happy Mother's Day/Father's Day/Birthday!

*****

Mum/Dad – you have always been my inspiration. You have shown me that it is possible to be, do or have whatever I set my mind to. You believe in me – thank you! Have a fabulous Mother's/Father's Day/Birthday.
You deserve the best!

*****

It is such a good feeling knowing that you are always there for me – thank you!

*****

I hope I know half as much as you when I'm a parent. Thank you for all your advice and support and unconditional love.

*****

The older I get, the more I value your wisdom and advice.
Thank you for guiding me in my decisions.

*****

Boss

You've been a wonderful boss. Thank you for providing great conditions and support throughout the year!

*****

It's a pleasure to work with you – thank you for being a wonderfully supportive boss.

*****

I enjoy coming to work because of the fun atmosphere. Thank you for creating such a positive environment in which to work.

*****

Staff

Thank you for your valued contribution. I really appreciate your input into the business.

*****

Thank you for your dedication to the business and your support of our objectives.

*****

A business is only as good as its staff. We are terrific and it's because of professional, caring and competent staff like you!

*****

Christmas

Jingle bells, jingle bells – Christmas time is here! Hope Santa is kind to you and you get everything your heart desires!

*****

As the Christmas lights twinkle and sparkle and remind us that there is brightness and hope in the world - I hope you and your family have a happy and peaceful Christmas.

*****

Jingle bells, jingle bells – Christmas time is here! May all the good will of Christmas be part of your home this festive season!

*****

May the joy, peace and goodwill that is Christmas, descend on your household and stay the whole year long.

*****

Merry Christmas and a happy and successful New Year! Enjoy the festivities and may you be renewed with a sense of happiness and contentment for the year ahead.

*****

Hope Santa is kind to you and delivers bundles of good health, wealth and happiness for the year ahead! Merry Christmas!

*****

Merry Christmas to you and your family – I hope you all have a wonderful time celebrating this special time of year and all that it means to you.

*****

Christening/Baby

As gently as an angel moves its wings of gossamer strands – the love you radiate for your baby girl will unite your hearts and hands.

*****

Special wishes for your little boy/girl on their christening/naming day.

*****

May the blessings from above flow down to them today and always.

*****

God Bless your son/daughter on their christening day! May the guidance and love from above be showered on them today.

*****

Welcome to your new baby! He'll/she'll fill your lives with love and heart warming experiences. Congratulations!

*****

Welcome to your precious bundle of joy! Babies multiply the love within a family. May your home overflow with happiness and wondrous experiences. Congratulations!

*****

So tiny, so perfect, so innocent! Congratulations on the new addition to your family. Life will never be the same! Enjoy the wonderful journey!

*****

Moving House

I hope you have lots of fun creating memories in your new home!

*****

Load up the furniture and the memories and enjoy the transition into your new home!

*****

Have fun settling into your new home! As you find places for all your belongings – leave room for the magical memories that will fill your home in the years ahead.

*****

A new house – a new adventure. New rooms to fill with love and new experiences. Enjoy the move and the time spent turning your new house into a home!

*****

Bereavement/ Loss/Goodbye

Though your 'loved one' has moved on – remember that memories last forever. These treasured moments will allow you to always keep them close to your heart.

*****

One door may have closed but remember – that out of this experience, new opportunities will emerge – often through unexpected doorways.

*****

I'm sending you loving thoughts in this difficult time.

*****

Words won't help ease your pain but I hope that knowing I am here for you and sending love and support may help you through this difficult time.

*****

Goodbye and good luck in your new venture – I hope you find all that you are searching for.

*****

Well the time has come to say 'goodbye' and looking back over the years we'll remember the times we've shared and we'll treasure every moment.

*****

Wherever you go may gentle winds follow and blow all your troubles away.

*****

Wherever you go may gentle winds be always at your back and blow you into safe harbours.

*****

Best wishes for your safe journey and may the 'angels' of travel guide you safely to your destination.

*****

Well the time has come to say goodbye – and looking back over the years we remember all the times we've shared – the successes, the challenges, the laughs, the sad times. You've been a helping hand to many - a constant, guiding light and your listening and caring ways set you apart as a great colleague and friend.

*****

He is with you in the gentle breath of the wind - He is with you in the warmth of the morning sun - He is with you in the waves breaking on the beach - He is with you in the twinkling of the stars…He is with you….He is with you….

*****

Our loved ones may leave this world but our memories will keep them nestled close in our hearts forever.

*****

If words could help take away your pain – we'd never stop our talking - If 'sharing' could ease your aching hearts – we'd walk the road you're walking - But we can only send our love to support you in these painful days - And hope you'll call us whenever you need anything– we're here for you.

*****

As he rises on the wings of angels into the arms of the Lord – be comforted – he is in kind and gentle hands.

*****

Be comforted in the knowledge that although not with us physically, our loved ones are always nestled close in our hearts and kept 'present' by our warmest memories.

*****

Good Luck

May the days ahead roll smoothly by bringing you exciting challenges and new opportunities.

*****

May new doors open to exciting experiences and success accompany you inside.

*****

May the blessings from above rain down on you today and always.

*****

Hope your day is filled with fun and special surprises! My wish for you is that in the year ahead you draw closer to your dreams.

*****

May the gentle winds of friendship always blow your troubles far away.

*****

Here's hoping that the year ahead is filled with nice surprises.

*****

As the doors open on a new year – may you walk through into the warmth of sunshine, the comfort of good health and the joy of true love!

*****

May the changing tides of fortune sweep you towards welcoming shores.

*****

Congratulations /Success /Achievement

Congratulations on your recent success.
May you use this experience to fire you up to go
on to bigger and better things in life.

*****

Congratulations on your recent promotion. Your diligence and commitment are an example to those around you. You are a great role model.

*****

You have left us a memory lane of magical moments – congratulations on your success and good luck in your new venture!

*****

We wish you well with the years ahead and all that you have planned. Your inspiring leadership and generous style have left their mark on all of us. You are the best!

*****

Your attitude to life inspires us – may your 'life rewards' all be 'gold'.

*****

Congratulations! You always were a star! Continue to 'shine' and inspire those around you.

*****

Wedding /Engagement

Congratulations on your engagement/marriage. May this be the beginning of a wonderful life of love, laughter and many magical moments.

*****

When two hearts collide like yours did – it is nature's way of saying you should be together forever!

*****

Although I can't be there to share in the happiness of your wedding day, my fondest thoughts are with you as I wish you both every joy and happiness for your future life together.

*****

Congratulations and our love and best wishes for a wonderful life together.

*****

The angel of love is watching over you today as you take this exciting step towards a combined future.

*****

Congratulations! You make a beautiful couple
– may you have an equally beautiful life together.

*****

Out with the 'me' and in with the 'we'! Congratulations
and best wishes for a life of sharing with, and
caring for, each other.

*****

Congratulations on making this important decision
– may your love grow daily and carry you through the
roller coaster of life.

*****

An angel is watching over you as you share your vows today – may that loving energy guide you to a happy and harmonious life together.

*****

Guidance /Inspiration /Friendship

You've been a helping hand to many – our shining guiding light. Your kindness and generosity are truly inspirational. Thank you for being such a great friend.

*****

I value your honesty and caring and your many other talents – you really are one of a kind.

*****

I know you're going through some tough times at the moment so I want you to know I'm here for you. I'm sending you positive thoughts – believe in yourself – times will get better!

*****

Years may pass but memories stay and our friendship's bonds are true.

*****

I want you to know that no matter what – I'll always be here for you - To listen, to support, to understand.

*****

Around good friends like you we feel at peace, despite life's trials and tribulations. True friends are hard to find and we're blessed to have you in our inner circle.

*****

You've empowered me to change my life – and take charge with positive action and I've learnt that I can steer my life in any direction at all.

*****

When times are tough and the cold hand of reality strikes, it's good to know you're there to support me. I'm grateful for the warmth of your friendship.

*****

There are times of trouble when we wander into strife and during these periods it's good to have a friend like you to help us through.

*****

We'll treasure the time we had with you - You are thought of often and held very close in a corner of our hearts.

*****

If you lose sight of your dreams….find a telescope.

*****

We would never appreciate the healing touch of raindrops if we had never experienced a drought…..

*****

Even though the night can be inky black and we can't see what lies before us, there is the certainty that morning <u>will</u> arrive and with it the promise of a 'sunrise' that will 'light up' the path ahead.

*****

Attitude is like ice-cream – it comes in many varieties and guess what? It's your choice what flavour you have!

*****

Belief is like the warmth of the winter sun –you can't 'see' it but you can feel it defrosting doubt and invigorating your soul.

*****

When times get tough, toughen up the time-keeper!

*****

Don't ever ask time to 'stand still' – just dance faster!

*****

The difference between a mistake and a lesson is how you handle the outcome.

*****

Commitment is the booster section in the rocket of your goals. When times get tough, it is your commitment to your job, to your partner or your team that sustains you and gives you the renewed energy to soar further through the universe of life.

*****

You may feel 'lonely' right now but remember, whilst you are in my thoughts and in my heart – you are never 'alone'.

*****

It's ok to cry. Tears are the soul's way of watering our memories. I'm here for you to help you bring back some sunshine into your life.

*****

Sometimes starting on a new journey can be scary because you can't see the end in sight. But remember – you only need to take the first step before the next one is revealed to you – and so it goes until before you know it – you have reached your destination.

*****

Thank You

Thank you for being there for me. When I need a 'listening' ear and a shoulder to lean on – you are always there.

You are a true friend.

*****

Thank you for your guidance and inspiration throughout the year.

*****

Thank you for caring – thank you for sharing. I treasure our times together and you will always have a special place in my heart.

*****

You have always been there – encouraging me, offering me your wisdom, listening to my fears – supporting me in every thing I do. Thank you. Your support has given me the strength to take on any challenge that has faced me.

*****

Thank you for sharing your experience and knowledge and helping to make me a better person/player etc

*****

You have been my 'lighthouse', my guiding light. I am so glad you are part of my life. Thank you.

*****

You really are a wonderful Dad – the best I could have chosen.

*****

A kaleidoscope of memories parades through my mind as I look back over the years and reflect on your many endearing qualities - thank you.

*****

We are sending our love for Father's Day along with a heartfelt 'thank you'!

*****

You've always been a special 'Dad' – the best
I could ever choose!

*****

Thank you for being a beautiful person from the inside
out – always loving and forever sharing.

*****

Thank you for your guidance and encouragement
– I appreciate it.

*****

Happy Birthday

Hope your day is filled with many magical moments.

*****

Have a wonderful day and here's hoping the years ahead
are filled with lots of love and laughter.

*****

Kick up your heels! Celebrate in style – you only live once!

*****

Special wishes for a special person! You deserve the best. Enjoy your day!

*****

Another year has passed – it's time to reflect on what you want from your future – today is the beginning of the rest of your life. Plan it wisely.

*****

Here's hoping that the year ahead is filled with nice surprises.

*****

Hope the coming year is filled with wonderful surprises and that you enjoy many magical moments.

*****

Hope you get spoilt rotten – you deserve to be!

*****

Hope all your birthday wishes come true!

*****

Relax and take it easy – this is YOUR day – spend it doing something YOU want to do!

*****

For twenty years we've shared your dreams, your hopes, your tears, and your 'FUN'! Now you've turned 21 and we look forward to sharing the next important phase of your life with you!

*****

Business Clients

Thank you for your business throughout the year.
Your support is truly appreciated.

*****

You are a valued client! Thank you for supporting us –
we look forward to being of further service
throughout the year.

*****

Your support of our services is truly valued.
Thank you!

*****

Thank you for supporting us throughout the year.
We have enjoyed our relationship with you and look
forward to adding further value to your business
in the coming year.

*****

Thank you for your patronage throughout the year.
We value your business and welcome your suggestions
as to how we can improve our service to
you in the years ahead.

*****

'Mix and Match' Support

Nouns

Angel	Dynamite	Knowledge	Plane	Solution	Wind
Arms	Energy	Lighthouse	Portfolio	Son	Wings
Baby	Expert	Lifetime	Pot of Gold	Soul-mate	Words
Bargain	Eyes	Look	Potential	Spotlight	World
Beauty	Face	Love	Power	Squad	You
Blast	Facts	Love of my life	Profits	Stars	
Bonanza	Fingers	Luxury	Quality	Stop	
Bonus	Formula	Magic	Rainbow	String	
Breeze	Fortune	Masterpiece	Reflections	Success	
Bundle of Joy	Friendship	Memory	Results	Sun	
Challenge	Fun	Miles	Rewards	Sunrise	
Child	Future	Mind	Road	Sunshine	
Class	Gallery	Miracle	Role model	Surprise	
Colours	Gift	Money	School	Sweetheart	
Concept	Guiding Light	Mum	Sampler	Talents	
Dad	Hand	Name	Secret	Team	
Daughter	Harvest	Opportunity	Shadows	Time	
Destination	Health	Partner	Ship	Tunes	
Destiny	Heart	Path	Skill	Water	
Dreams	Journey	Personal	Sky	Wealth	

Adjectives

Affordable	Discount	Fun	Lively	Reduced	Thrilling
Alert	Distinguished	Genuine	Lowest	Reliable	Timely
Alluring	Easy	Gigantic	Magical	Remarkable	Tremendous
Amazing	Effective	Greatest	Mammoth	Revolutionary	Ultimate
Attractive	Electrifying	Helpful	Mind Blowing	Rewards	Unconditional
Authentic	Energizing	Highest	Miracle	Savvy	Unique
Beautiful	Enjoyable	Hot	Monumental	Seductive	Useful
Big	Enormous	Huge	Mouth-watering	Sensational	Valuable
Challenging	Enterprising	Important	New	Shocking	Vital
Colourful	Excellent	Improved	Odd	Sizzling	Vivid
Colossal	Exciting	Incredible	Old	Special	Winning
Competitive	Exclusive	Informative	Popular	Strange	Wonderful
Complete	Expert	Innovative	Powerful	Strong	
Comprehensive	Explode	Insatiable	Practical	Stunning	
Confidential	Explosive	Instructive	Professional	Sturdy	
Crucial	Famous	Interesting	Profitable	Successful	
Daring	Fascinating	Largest	Promising	Superior	
Dazzling	Flourishing	Latest	Proven	Surging	
Delicious	Fortunate	Liberated	Quick	Surprising	
Direct	Free	Limited	Rare	Terrific	

Verbs

Accomplish	Dare	Focus	Listen	Reflect	Stretch
Achieve	Discover	Follow	Live	Relax	Strum
Air	Dream	Gaze	Look	Remember	Support
Approved	Drown	Go	Lose	Remind	Sweep
Attain	Ease	Grasp	Love	Reveal	Take
Believe	Emerge	Guide	Made	Rise	Taught
Blow	Empower	Handle	Move	Roll	Teach
Break	Encourage	Help	Need	Run	Thank
Bound	Engulf	Hide	Nestle	Say	Touch
Breathe	Enjoy	Hold	Obtain	See	Treasure
Bring	Envision	Hope	Open	Send	Twinkle
Call	Excite	Imagine	Pass	Set	Trust
Celebrate	Experience	Increase	Picture	Sit	Uncover
Challenge	Explode	Inspire	Plan	Share	Understand
Change	Explore	Keep	Promise	Shine	Unite
Close	Fill	Know	Protect	Sparkle	Unleash
Collide	Find	Last	Radiate	Spoil	Unwrap
Compare	Fire	Learn	Rain	Start	Use
Create	Flourish	Leave	Reach	Steer	Value
Dance	Fly	Light	Reap	Stop	Walk

About the Author

Author, Essential Oil Mentor, International Speaker and Mindset Educator, Lover of People and Life!

After life-saving treatment from the Royal Flying Doctor Service when living in the outback of Australia, Leonie's purpose in life has always been to give back to the community.

With an employment record closely resembling a patchwork quilt, she became passionately self-employed building direct sales teams, consulting to companies and delivering tailor-made corporate training solutions nationally and internationally.

Today, Leonie's teachings are delivered on a platform of aromatic essences as she combines facts, humour and inspiration to inform, educate and inspire others to implement immediate changes to their lives by bringing more health and harmony into each day with balanced holistic health practises and doTERRA® Essential Oils.

Along the way Leonie has authored two books:
A Way With Words—
Sentiments for all Occasions
and
How To Get More Done In Your Day

There are more in the pipeline as she fulfills her purpose to empower others to Come To Their Senses and Become The Best They Can Be!

www.ingramcontent.com/pod-product-compliance
Lightning Source LLC
Chambersburg PA
CBHW070311010526
44107CB00056B/2557